GW01375527

DANCE

© Rupa Classic India Series 1993
First published 1993 by Rupa & Co.
7/16 Ansari Road, Daryaganj, New Delhi-110 002
Second impression 1998
Set in 9.6 on 12 Palatino by Fototype, New Delhi
Printed in India by R.N. Polyplast Pvt. Ltd., Noida

ISBN 81-7167-207-8

Photographs on pages 5, 20, 21, 37, 40, 49, 51, 53, 59, 61-64 courtesy MOHAN KHOKAR DANCE COLLECTION

Design: KD Prashad
General Editor: Amrita Kumar

DANCE

Text and photographs by
Ashish Khokar

Rupa & Co

INTRODUCTION

The gods created dance as a device for entertainment. Later, in order to please the gods, human beings enacted the tale and glory of the gods. Thus began a cycle of celebration manifested in the joyous abandon of movement and music. Over a period of two millennia, dance in India acquired a set grammar, which led to a certain codification of technique. Thus were sown the seeds for Bharata Muni's celebrated treatise on dance, the Natyashastra. *This was complemented with an accelerated manifestation of formalised religion through the temple. In the temples, the art of dance evolved to its pristine glory, offered as it were to the gods. The kings were patrons of various art forms and thus the court, too, played an important role in the promotion and propagation of dance.*

With new cultural influences in the past millennia, a fusion and synthesis came about. The traditions of central Asia were absorbed in the repertoire of dance which partly left its moorings in the temple and moved to the court. The colonial rule of India led to the slow demise of classical dance which when the country gained Independence were revived. The spirit of rejuvenation has helped Indian classical dance attain an important place in world culture.

Saraswati, the goddess of arts and higher knowledge, in an Orissi projection by dancer Protima Gauri Bedi.

Cover: *The theme of Krishna, enacted through Krishnattam, performed by only one group in the country, affiliated to the Guruvayoor temple in Kerala.*

KATHAK

The origins of Kathak can be ascribed to the tradition of katha or the art of story-telling. Developed initially as an offering to the gods, this dance form soon came under the influence of the Mughal court. Thus emerged the Lucknow gharana or school, distinct from the Jaipur school which focused on stories of Rajput valour and popular gods.

The Jaipur school emphasizes technical accomplishment, rhythmic footwork and circular pirouettes while the Lucknow school focuses on expressional work and shows traces of Muslim court etiquette. But in both, the theme of Radha-Krishna is central. Additions to the style have come through the Benaras school, which has charted an independent course.

Kathak has benefited immensely from the Kalka-Bindadin family of the Lucknow gharana and the Gangani and Lal brothers, after Sundar Prasad, in the Jaipur mould. As a classical dance form it lends itself well to solo, duet and group compositions. Referred to as nautch under colonial rule, Kathak has come of age in independent India and forms the core of classical dance language in north, west and central India. Sitara Devi, Damayanti Joshi, Roshan Kumari, Birju Maharaj and Kumudini Lakhia are some of its seasoned exponents.

Kathak regales with its rhythmic footwork and circular pirouettes. Dancer Sharmistha Mukherjee undertakes one such swirling chakra with gay abandon.

The concept of **salaami** *or salutations is integral to Kathak, especially the Lucknow school. Harish Rawat and Sharmistha Mukherjee welcome the audience in a customary gesture earlier made to the king, nobility or the patron.*

Here they represent the Muslim concept of purdah *and the Hindu tradition of* ghoongat.

The bareequi *or delicateness of the wrist and eye movements are shown here by Sharmistha Mukherjee.*

Performing symbolic rituals in front of deities of the Hindu pantheon, Harish Rawat undertakes a typical stance of obeisance.

Nazar-andaaz *or eye movement and gaze-appeal come through in an intense projection by the legendary Sitara Devi, the reigning queen of Kathak at seventy years of age.*

Right : *Harish Rawat in preparation of the* chakra *or circular movements which manifest in mutiples of three and can continue upto 108!*

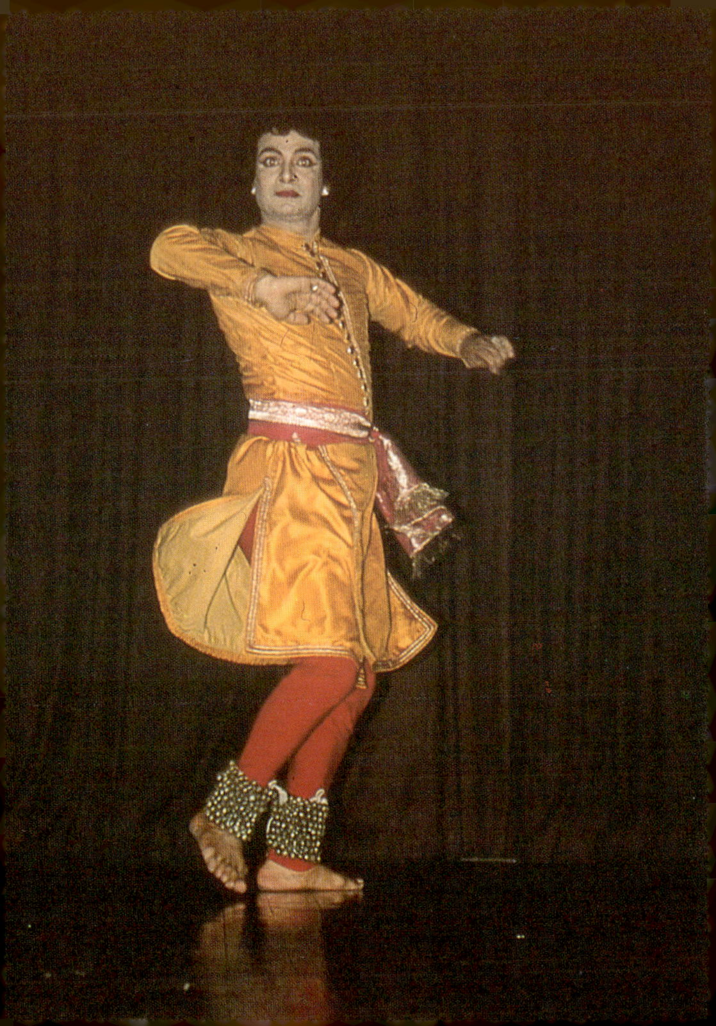

BHARATA NATYAM

Bharata Natyam originated in Tamil Nadu. It is one of the oldest of the Indian classical dance forms. The words Bharata Natyam comprise bha *for* bhava *or expression;* ra *for* raga *or musical mode and* ta *for* tala *or rhythm. Natyam means the art of dance.*

As an art-offering to the temple deities, this form ushered in the custom of temple servitors called devadasis *who danced only for the gods. With the passage of time and corrupting cultural influences, as also changes in patronage and promotion, the* devadasis *came to be associated with those serving men, not gods. This malady was set right only in the early part of the present century when the* devadasi *system was abolished.*

The next phase, around Independence, saw the restoration and resurgence of the dance form. It came to be associated with a new class of practitioners, the Brahmins, who gave it respectability. The efforts of E Krishna Iyer, Prof. Sambhamoorthy and Rukmini Devi Arundale helped the art of gurus like Meenakshi Sundaram Pillai and Kattumanar Koil Muthukumara Pillai reach several disciples who became stars of the form: Ram Gopal, Mrinalini Sarabhai, M K Saroja and Kamala. The generation thereafter, Yamini Krishnamurthy, Padma Subramanyam and Sonal Mansingh helped it attain popularity.

In a celebration of female energy or shakti, *Geeta Chandran represents Durga.*

The grammar of Bharata Natyam is composed of adavus or body positions. Geeta Chandran depicts an alapadma sequence.

Right : Mythology forms the basis of Indian classical dance. Here the dancer represents Parvati, the consort of Shiva.

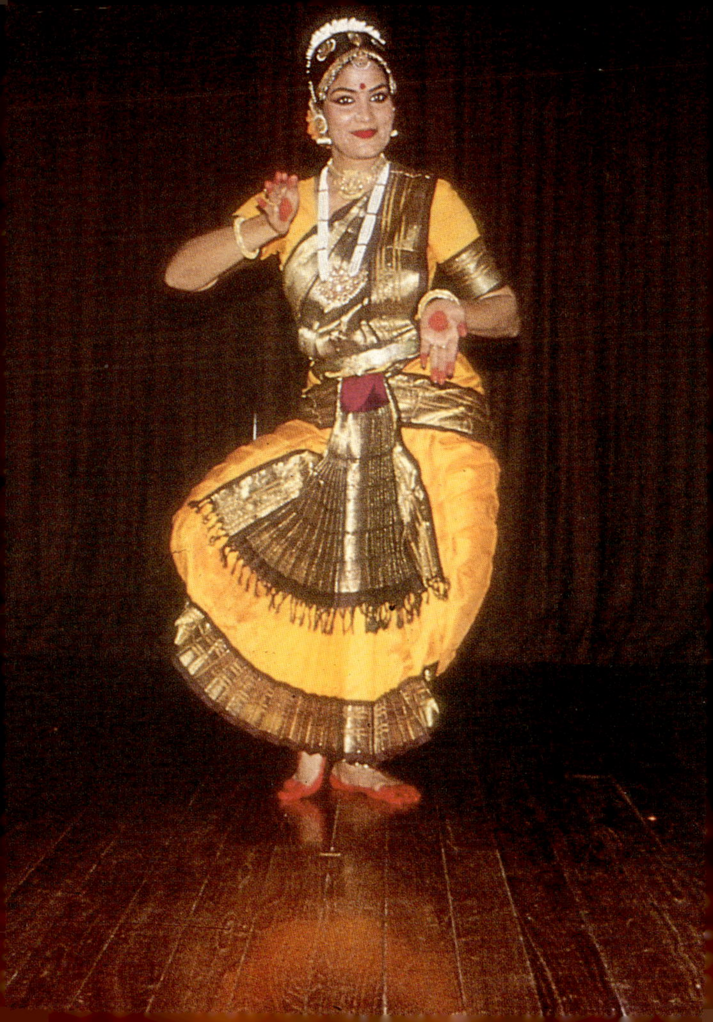

Another form of female energy is Meenakshi, also known as Parvati or Durga.

Hand gestures or hastas *form the core of dance language in Bharata Natyam. Shown here is* kapita hasta.

Nritta *or the pure technical aspect of dance forms the foundation of this form. Sonal Mansingh in a frozen sequence.*

Here she supplements body positions with hand gestures or hastas.

Integral to the classicism of Bharata Natyam is its devotional content. Bhakti bhava *represented by a veteran exponent of* Bhakti abhinaya, M K Saroja.

Here she depicts fear, one among the nine sentiments or navarasa.

MOHINI ATTAM

The state of Kerala offers a rich kaleidoscope of dance forms. Mohini Attam forms the core of this offering. It is hailed as the dance of the enchantress or the celestial nymph, Mohini, who enticed the gods. In her honour, this dance form was created and formalised in the eighteenth century.

Mohini Attam catered to both god and man, taking some features from Bharata Natyam and Kathakali, the powerful classical dance-drama of Kerala. While Kathakali is traditionally performed only by men, Mohini Attam is performed by women. With its lyrical prose accompaniment and leitmotif of feminine charm it enraptures audiences.

The Mohini Attam repertoire consists of five principal items, starting with cholkettu, *then* varnam, jatiswaram, padam *and concluding with* tillana. *The graceful movements are offset by an austere white sari with a gold or red border. Typical to the ornamentation is the hair-bun, made on the left side. Gold ornaments on the neck, waist, wrist and ankle bells complete the attire of this celestial enchantress. Kanak Rele, Kshemavati, Bharati Shivaji and Deepti Omchery Bhalla are well-known exponents of the form.*

With Cupid's arrow pointed at the Lord, dancer Kshemavati brings out the essence of the style.

Deepti Omchery Bhalla depicts the opening of the lotus bloom, symbolizing desire and growing beauty.

Here she is in a typical knee-bent, legs-extended position.

KATHAKALI

To the lush green of Kerala belongs Kathakali, a powerful dance-drama which captures the courage of heroic kings and the cunning of evil characters. Its elaborate and colourful facial make-up takes upto six hours to prepare: green is for heroic characters like Rama and Krishna; black for evil characters like Putana and the bearded countenance depicts Hanuman and Bheema. Traditionally, only men perform Kathakali, undertaking the role of women too. Their training includes elaborate eye exercises, body massage and diet control.

Kathakali is based mostly on mythology and the themes of Rama and Krishna. It is performed in the precincts of the temple and is episodic in character, with a single story stretching to several consecutive nights of performance. Loud drum playing invites audiences from neighbouring villages.

As a distinct form, Kathakali evolved from Krishnattam, Ramanattam, Koodiyattam, Mudeyyetu and Teyyam. At the hands of the poet Vallathol, it received a shot in the arm in the creation of the institution called Kalamandalam. Some well-known exponents of Kathakali are Guru Gopinath, Guru Krishnan Nair, Gopi of Kalamandalam and Sadanam Balakrishnan.

Details of make-up and ornaments, including the elaborate head-gear.

From the story of Duryodhana Vadham, where Bheema in the guise of a cook slays the evil king.

Right : *The* stree vesham *or female impersonation.*

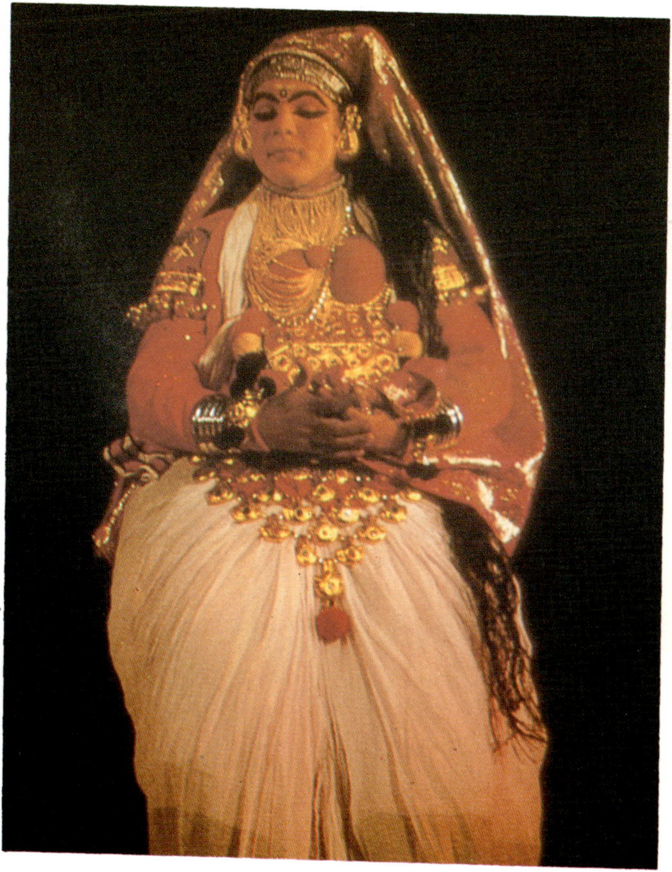

The bearded Hanuman symbolises the merry mischief of the monkey-king from the Ramayana.

Right : *Krishnattam, the form which preceded Kathakali focuses on the theme of Krishna, the blue god. This form is rare and performed only by the troupe of the Guruvayoor temple in Kerala.*

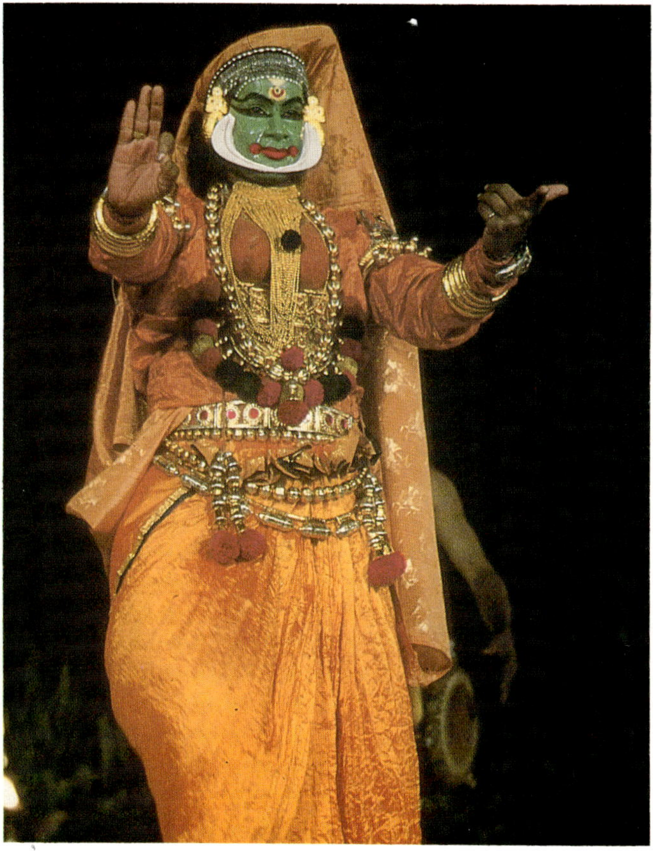

Ramanattam preceded Krishnattam and focuses on the theme of Rama. The use of a wooden mask as against the painted face of the Kathakali performer is a notable difference.

Right : *Teyyam means* daivam. *It is a ritual form of dance-drama performed only on particular religious occasions.*

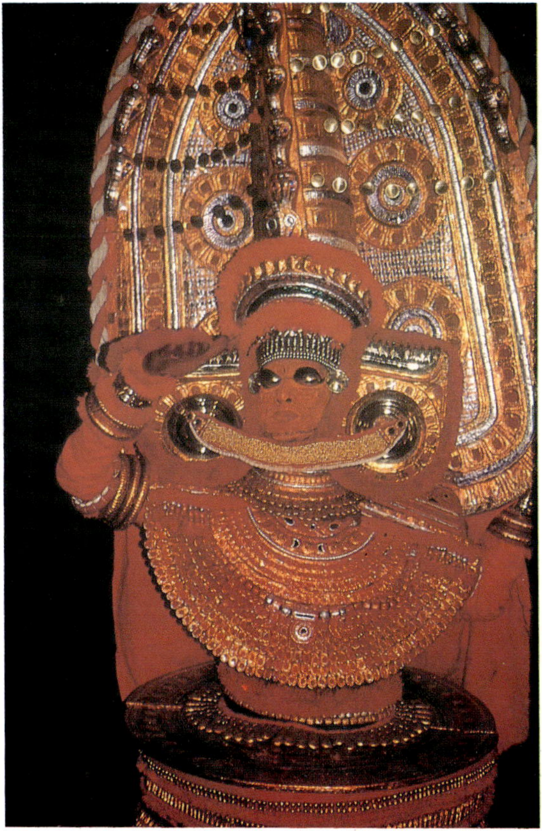

KUCHIPUDI

Hailing from the village of this name, in the Krishna district of Andhra Pradesh, Kuchipudi stemmed from the Bhakti (or devotional) movement of the sixth century. However, its present form was attained in the middle of the seventeenth century, after its progenitor, Siddendra Yogi undertook to present the love of Satyabhama for Krishna. With the specific purpose of raising the form above the reach of the devadasis, he used Brahmin boys to enact the role.

Kuchipudi developed into a very popular theatre art requiring a set of characters. It was never intended to be a solo dance as is common in the present times. Traditionally, the performers were men or young boys. A sutradhar or anchor-person connects the theme in presentation. The expressional items project songs in Telugu or Sanskrit, with material borrowed from several sources.

Kuchipudi is fast-paced, with emphasis on the erotic. It is dance that is also drama, for the performer acts and speaks as well. Since Independence, the form has moved out of its native Andhra. The names of Yamini Krishnamurthy, Raja and Radha Reddy and Swapnasundari, after the work of Gurus Vempati Chinna Satyam, Guru Pasumarthi and Vedantam Satya Narayan, are synoymous with the style.

Kala Krishna, male performer of Kuchipudi, in a female role. Kuchipudi was traditionally the preserve of men.

The letters of Satyabhama to Lord Krishna form a theme in Kuchipudi. Kala Krishna depicts Satyabhama.

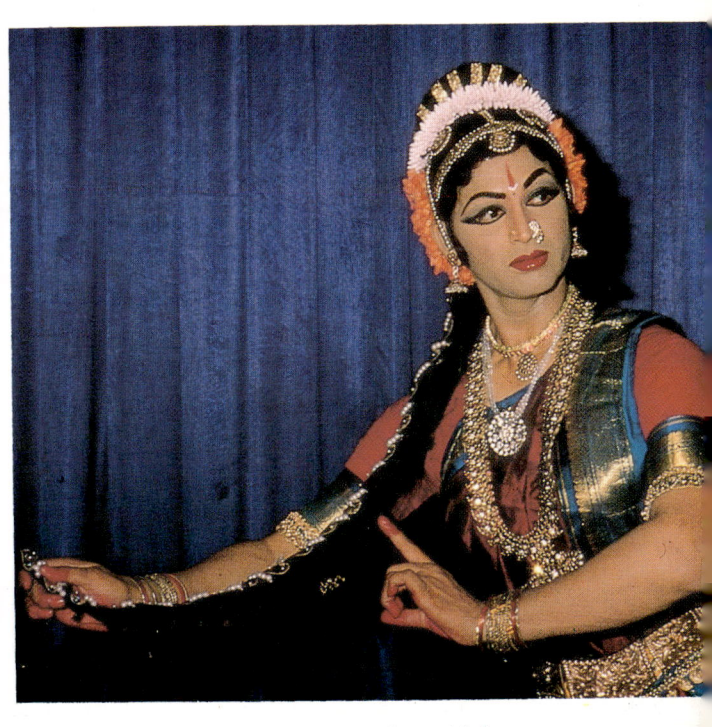

The impersonation of women is complete with long tresses, adding feminine charm.

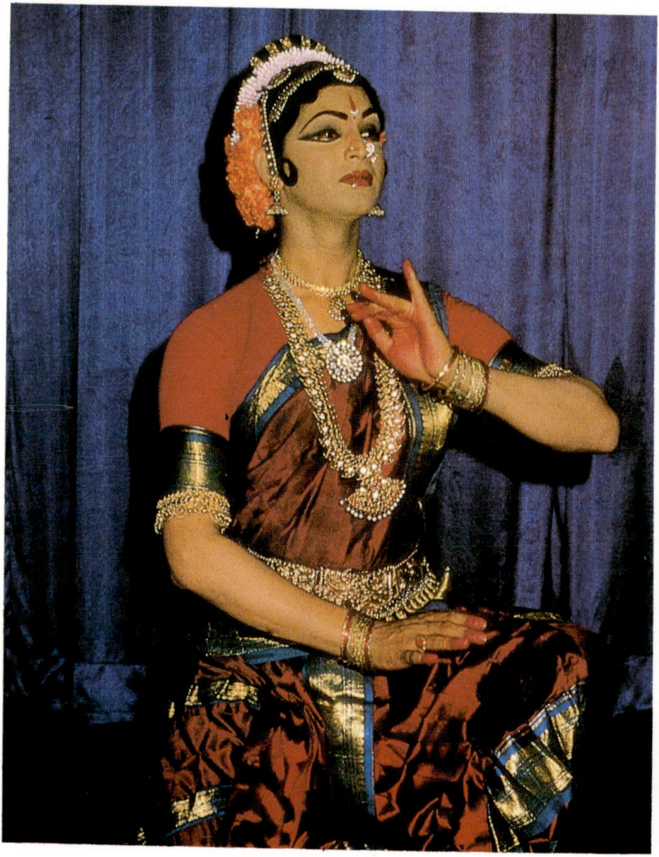

From amongst the few traditional performing families of this dance form, Vithal Pasumarthi represents a long lineage of renowned artistes.

Left : *Here Kala Krishna suggests the pride of place occupied by a proud Satyabhama, queen-consort of Krishna.*

The nritta *or technical aspect of Kuchipudi brought to life by the duo Vithal-Bharti.*

Kuchipudi delights in exaggerated abhinaya. *This gives the form a folk flavour.*

ORISSI

Orissi hails from the state of Orissa. At once sensuous and spiritual, it has the ability to manifest erotic sentiment in a deeply reverential manner. It celebrates the love of Radha and Krishna, the supreme soul-mates as immortalised in the Geet Govinda, *the mystic-erotic poem by Jayadeva.*

With the construction of the Jagannath temple in the early twelfth century, the practice of dedicating dancing girls or maharis *in the service of the temple was initiated. In the early seventeenth century, a class of boys dressed up as girls performed at the temples and in akhadas or gymnasia. Their dance was lively, combining as it did nritta elements with acrobatic elements. The Orissi dance absorbed a good deal from this gotipua style. Today the* maharis *and the gotipua boys are gone but Orissi has come of age. It was with the efforts of dance-historians and critics like Charles Fabri, Mohan Khokar and Dr Mayadhar Mansinha, noted litterateur and poet of Orissa that Orissi as a dance form came to be accepted widely. Gurus like Pankaj Charan Das, Deba Prasad Das, Kelucharan Mahapatra and Mayadhar Raut gave the form its structure and in the hands of their disciples the art gained recognition. Indrani Rehman's role in giving Orissi a national and international profile is unmatched. Sanjukta Panigrahi, Aloka Panikar, Kum Kum Mohanty, Kiran Segal, Madhavi Mudgal and Protima Bedi have promoted the form further.*

From the Geet Govinda, *Ambikaa Paniker depicts a* nayika *or love-lorn maiden in a pensive mood.*

Manglacharan *is the opening salutory item in Qrissi. Ambikaa Paniker depicts Saraswati, goddess of learning.*

Here she represents pallavi, *which in Orissi means elaboration of pure technical dance.*

Ambikaa Paniker in a sequence from the Geet Govinda *describing the slaying of the demon Keshi by Krishna.*

In the seventeenth century the gotipua boys delighted in acrobatic feats, providing entertainment as part of the Orissi tradition.

MANIPURI

Literally meaning "gem country", Manipur was founded on Parvati's order to Shiva to discover a place where they could dance like Krishna did with his gopis, legend says. Since then, the Manipuris have been celebrating with religious fervour their love for life. From this part in the extreme northeast of India hails the classical dance Manipuri.

The Lai Haroba or frolic of the gods, is the popular expression of dance in the month of May-June. It is a ceremonial offering in which the old and young, men and women participate. Popular Meithei legends like the love-tale of Khamba-Tobi are woven in. With the passage of history, kings and times, the Raas and Sankeertan were introduced. The Manipuri Raas focuses on the Radha-Krishna theme. There are different types of Raas, linked with the seasons. Sankeertan, derived from congregational singing, took two distinct forms: Poong Cholam and Kartal Cholam. While the Poong is danced with drums, the Kartaal has huge metal cymbals adorned with trailing red tassels. Besides maintaining the rhythm, these cymbals enhance the musicality of the peformance, ending in a crescendo. Another form is the Goshta Leela, where young boys participate. The stories pertain to the childhood of Krishna.

The work of Guru Bipin Singh, Princess Binodini, the Jhaveri sisters and Singhajit-Charu Singh has helped the form reach far and wide beyond its home-setting.

Traditional Manipuri Raas performed in the precincts of the temple. The dancers represent gopis. The ornamented and starched skirts are typical to the style.

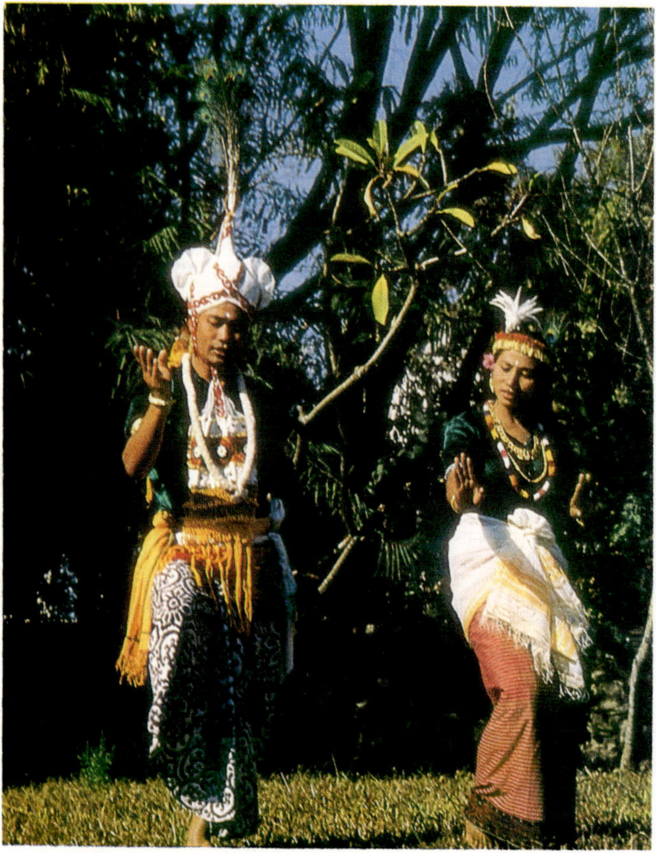

The Poong Cholam or the drum dance which forms part of the ritualistic congregational offering.

Left : The tragic tale of the lovers Khamba-Tobi is enacted here.

YAKSHAGANA

Yakshagana hails from the coastal strip of Karnataka. There is evidence in the **Bharatatesha Vaibha** *(written in 1557 A.D.) that this form is at least 400 years old. Yakshagana has its base in the ritualistic* **Nagamandala** *practices. The heart of this form is* **gana** *or song, arising from a distinct class of Kannada literature. Practically every theme carries a moral.*

Yakshagana is actually dance-opera. A play has 200 to 300 stanzas set to various metres. The **bhagvata** *or the conductor of the dance-opera first sings a verse and the characters interpret it through expressional dance. Some 150* **ragas** *are known to the Yakshagana tradition. The principal manifestations are of Vishnu. The active performance season is from December to May, when the crop has been harvested.*

Dancing in Yakshagana is not very intricate which is why it is sometimes mistaken or relegated to folk theatre. Footwork is very important, though **hasta** *or hand gestures are near absent.* **Aharya** *or make-up in this form is distinctive as in Kathakali. The characters are divided into certain principal types. Noble kings have a large black moustache and a sacred red mark on the forehead. A gilded crown adds appeal to kings and heroes. Performers are mostly villagers.*

The role of a king or a nobleman performed by a moustachioed actor. Note the lower garment, the dhoti, in red and yellow checks, very typical of the Yakshagana costume.

Elaborate, gilded headgear denoting royal and heroic characters.

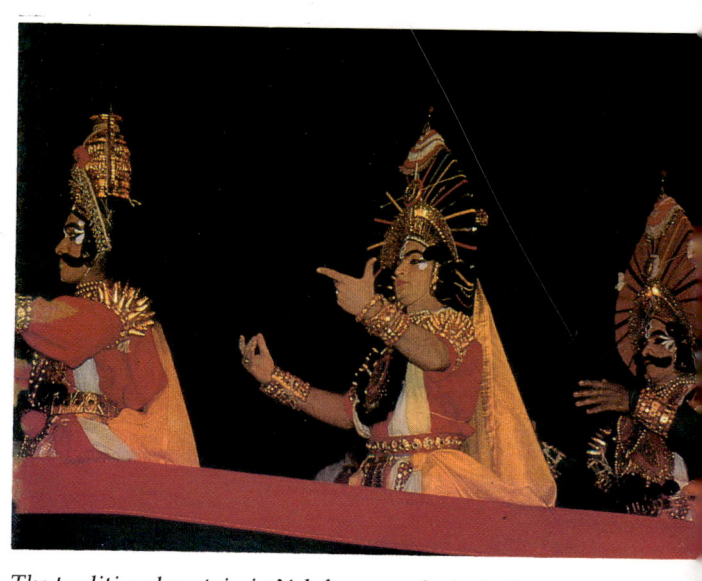

The traditional curtain in Yakshagana which divides time and different acts of the play.

SATRIYA

The principal form of classical dance in Assam is the Satriya. Although throughout its ancient history, as recorded by travellers like Hieun-Tsang and others, this land prided itself on dances like Nati and Ojapali, it was only with the birth of Sankaradeva in the mid-fifteenth century that a clear classical form emerged. Possessed as he was with religious fervour, Sankaradeva presented performances all over India, against painted backdrops. Essentially these dances related to the Vishnu cult and Sankaradeva was trying to cajole a corrupt and degraded society out of slumber. He himself participated as Vishnu. This form, the Chinna Yatra became the starting point for the emergence of a new and distinct genre which came to be called Ankia Nat.

Celibate monks form the core of participants of the form. Krishna, as an incarnation of Vishnu is the most celebrated figure. The philosophy of Sankaradeva is crystallised in the six works he wrote which now form the basis of Ankia Nat. These plays are performed in **satras**, *or schools for scriptural learning. Hence the name, Satriya.*

A celibate monk in the garb of a sutradhar *or anchor-person.*

CHHAU

The word Chhau is derived from chhaya *or shadow or mask, which is integral to two of the three forms of Chhau. Originally hailing from one belt, in independent India its home-ground was distributed to the three adjoining states of Bihar, Orissa and Bengal. In Bihar, the Seraikella royalty preserved, projected and participated in Chhau, in the month of Chaitra Parv, April. A characteristic of this form is the use of masks to convey moods.*

Mayurbhanj Chhau hails from Orissa, from a district of that name. It has vigour and aplomb, a feature shared with Seraikella Chhau. Both contain an element of mock combat. But while the Seraikella uses masks, Mayurbhanj does not. The technique of Chhau incorporates pharikhandas, *a system of exercises which was important in the training of soldiers and which accounts for its martial spirit. The themes are taken from mythology and in this the Purulia Chhau of Bengal holds a special place. It has only one message: the triumph of good over evil. Fighting dominates.*

The costumes are rich, full of tinsel and beads and peacock plumes. A colourful spectacle, the Chhau dance calls for great energy and, at the same time, control. The rendering can be very dignified, done as it is with ritualistic fervour and refrain.

Radha and Krishna with masks and attire in Seraikella Chhau. Performed by the royal family of Seraikella.

The pharikhanda *exercises lend martial vigour to the form, as seen here in Seraikella Chhau.*

The Purulia Chhau of West Bengal as performed by this highly decorated dancer.

A dance of a devoted mendicant as represented in Mayurbhanj Chhau.